Interior Design Coloring Book

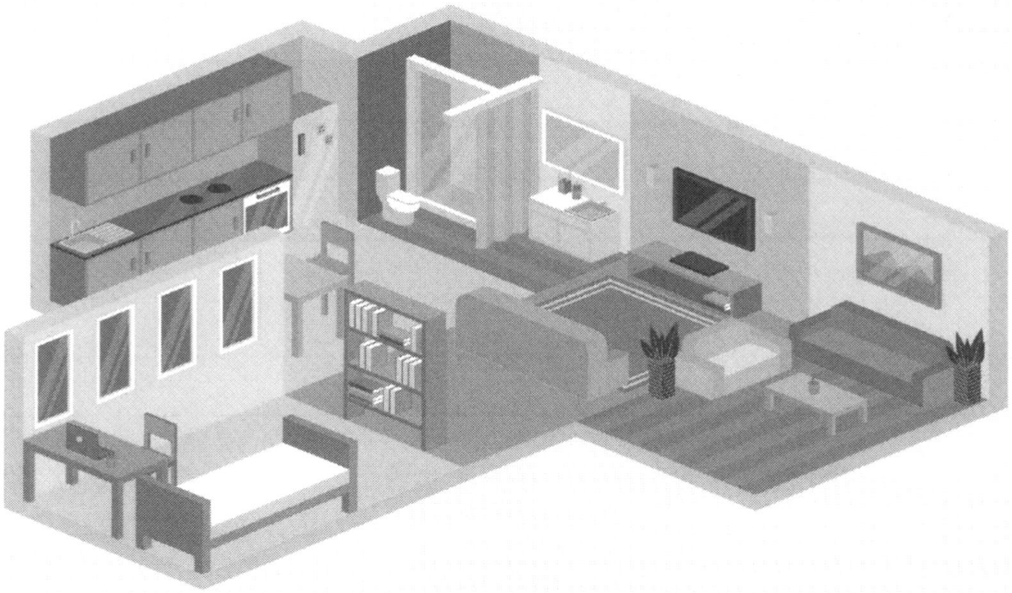

This Coloring Book Belongs To:

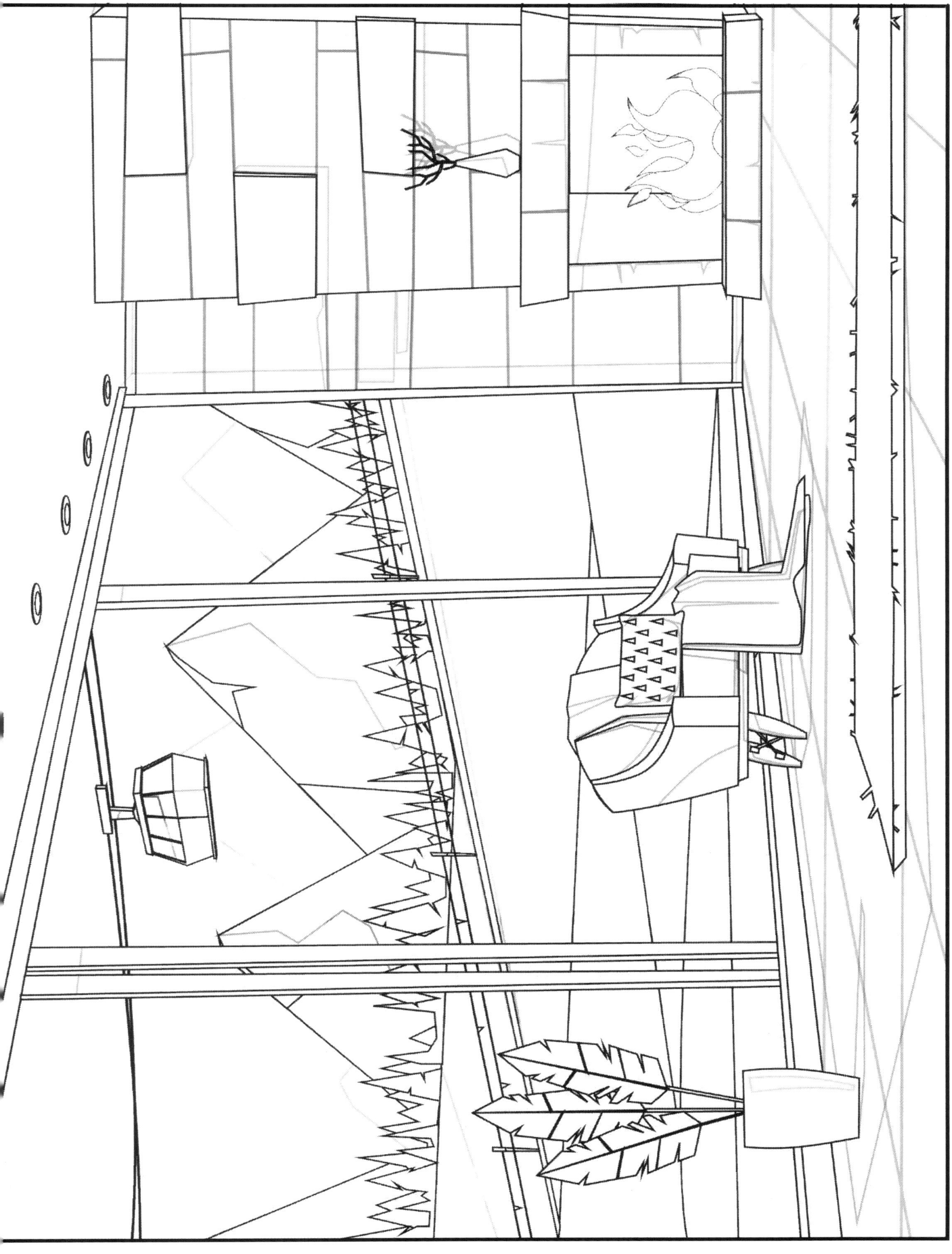

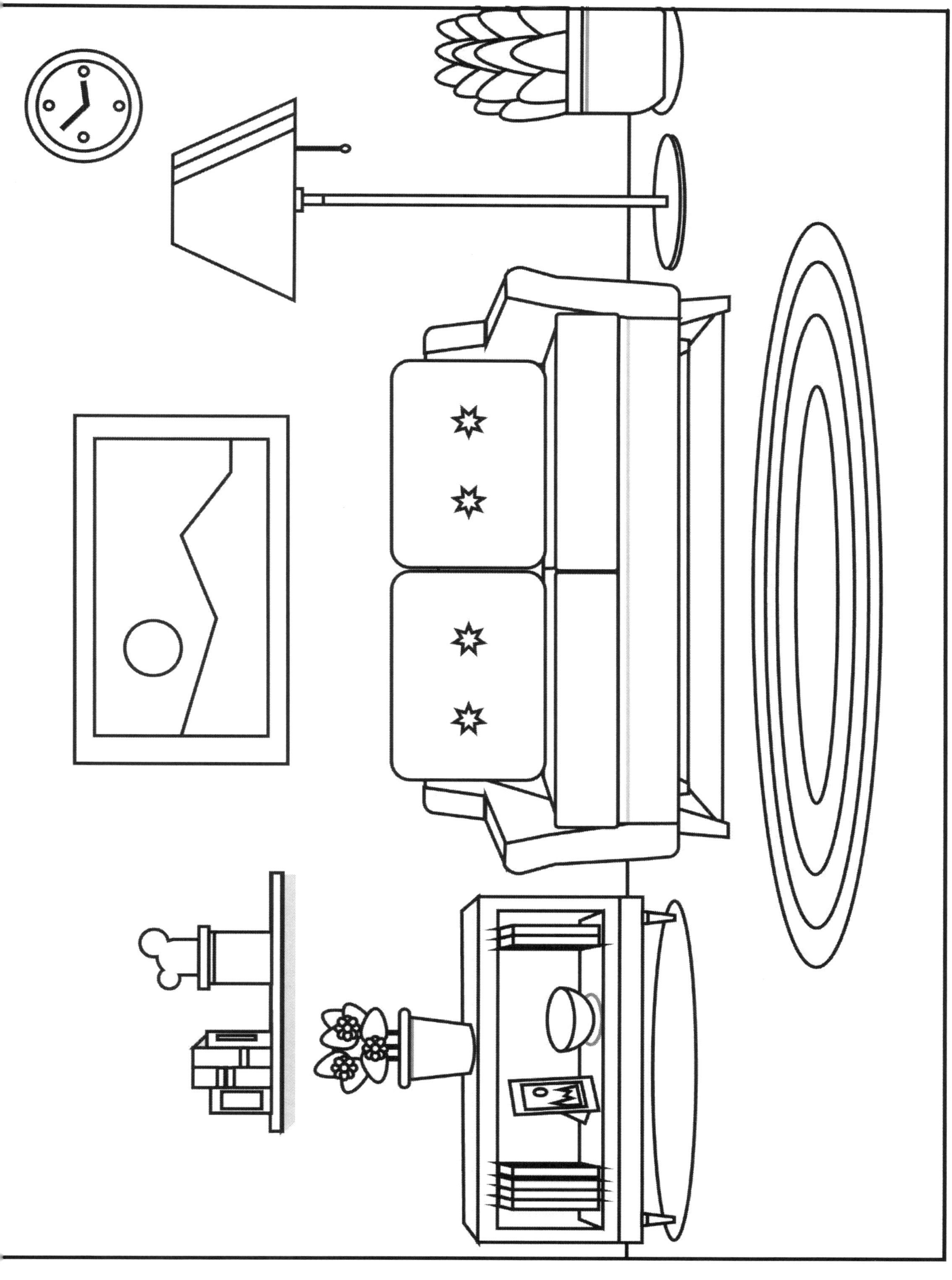

When you lose,
don't lose the
lesson.

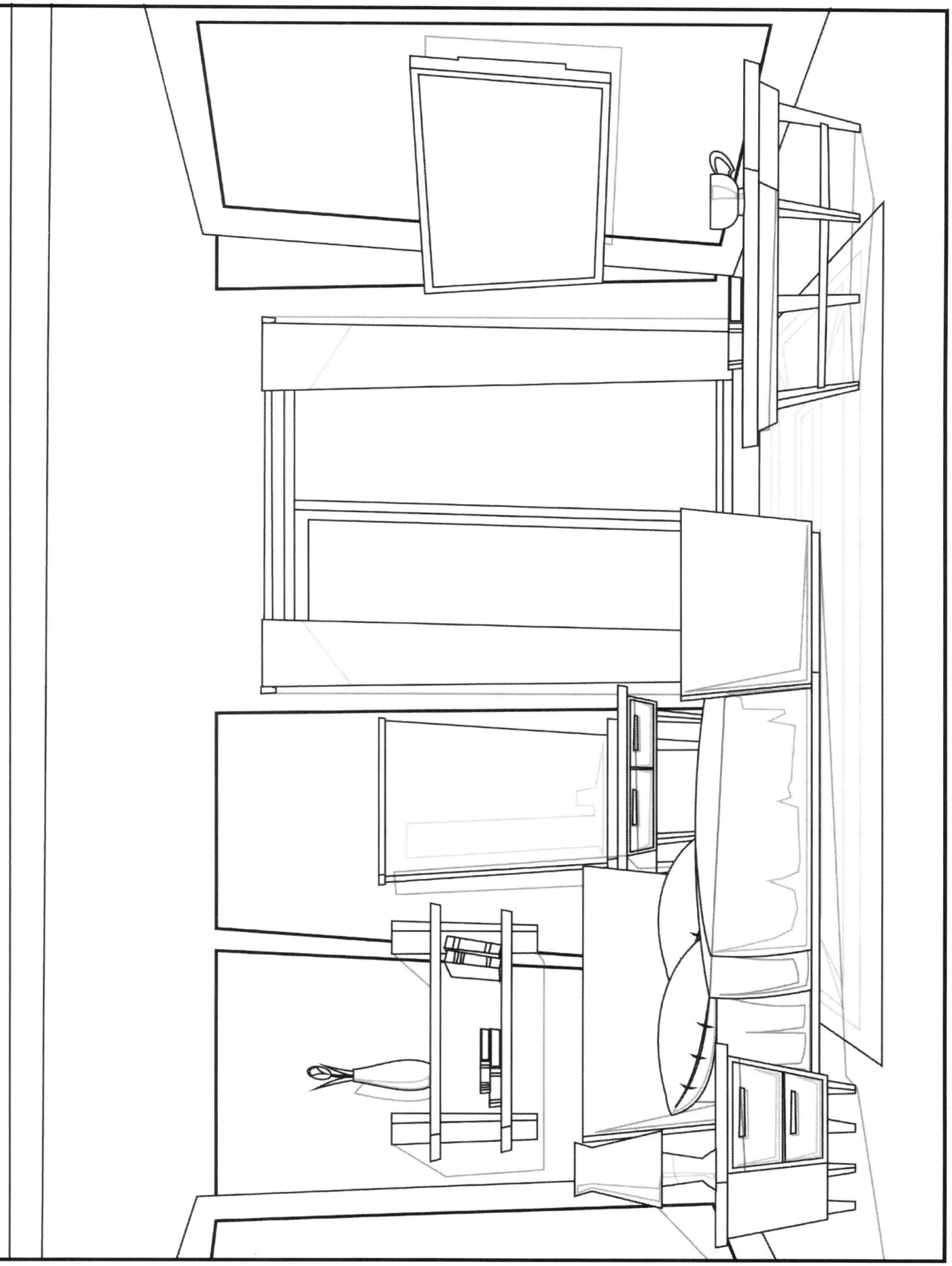

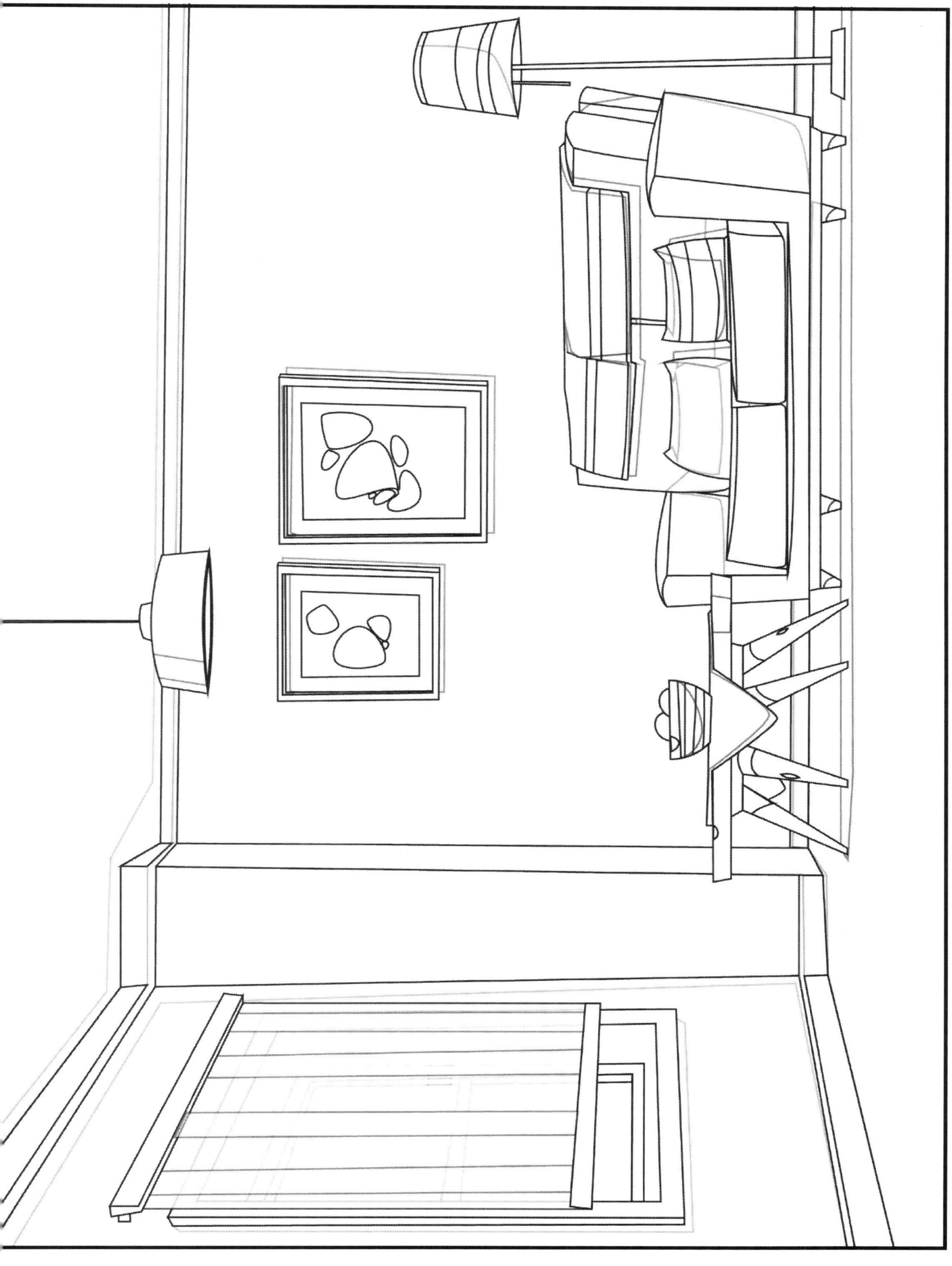

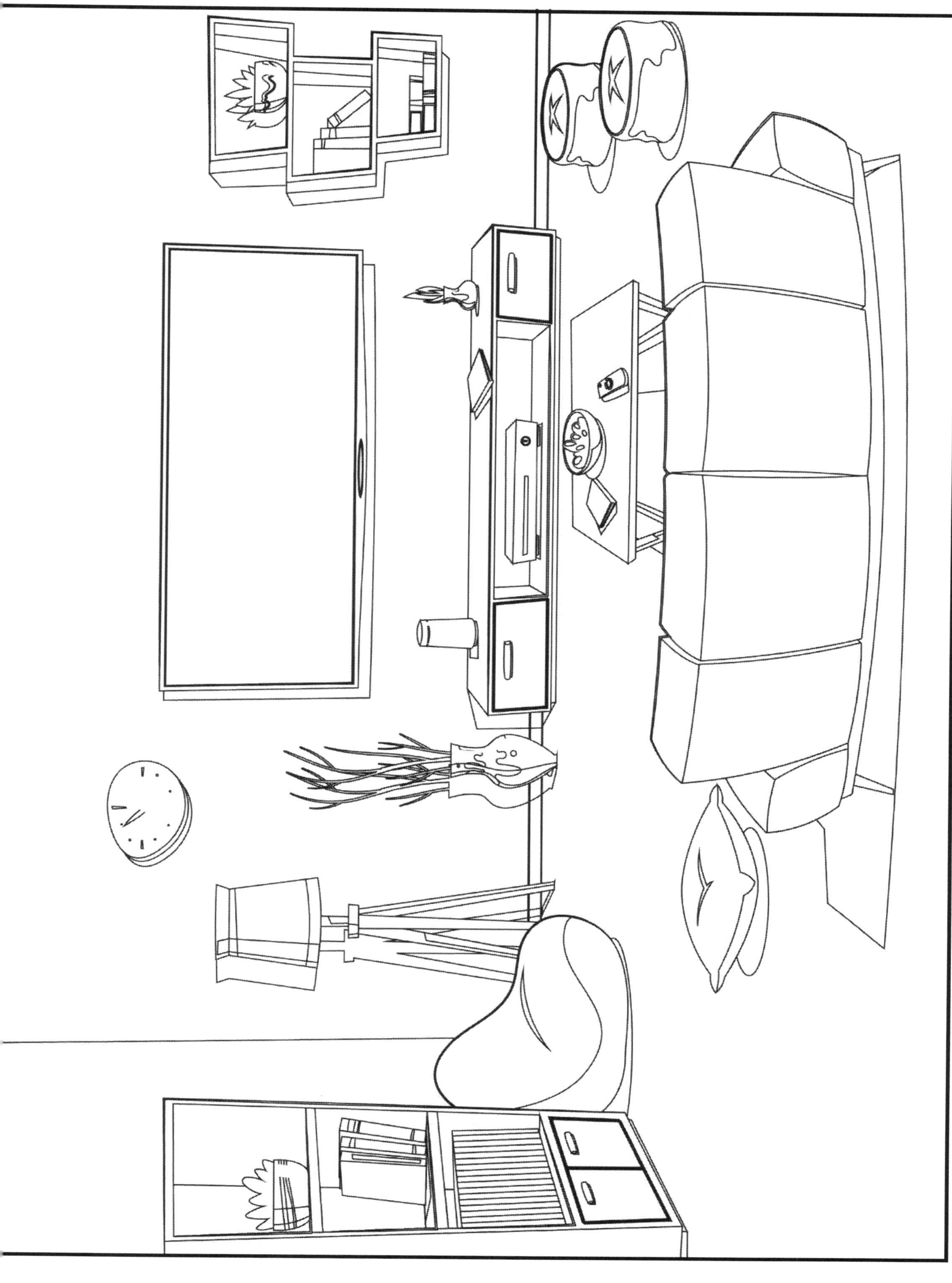

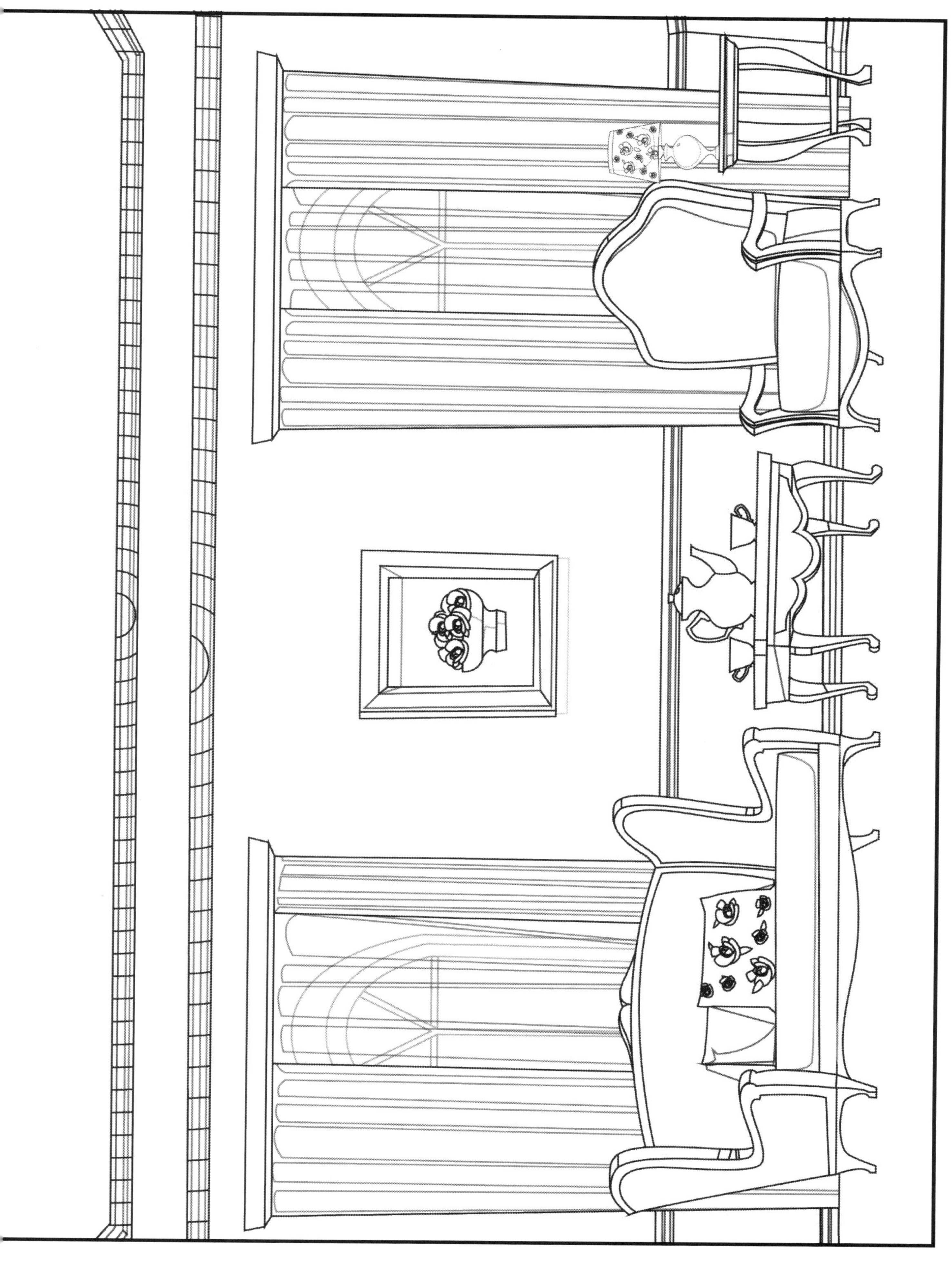

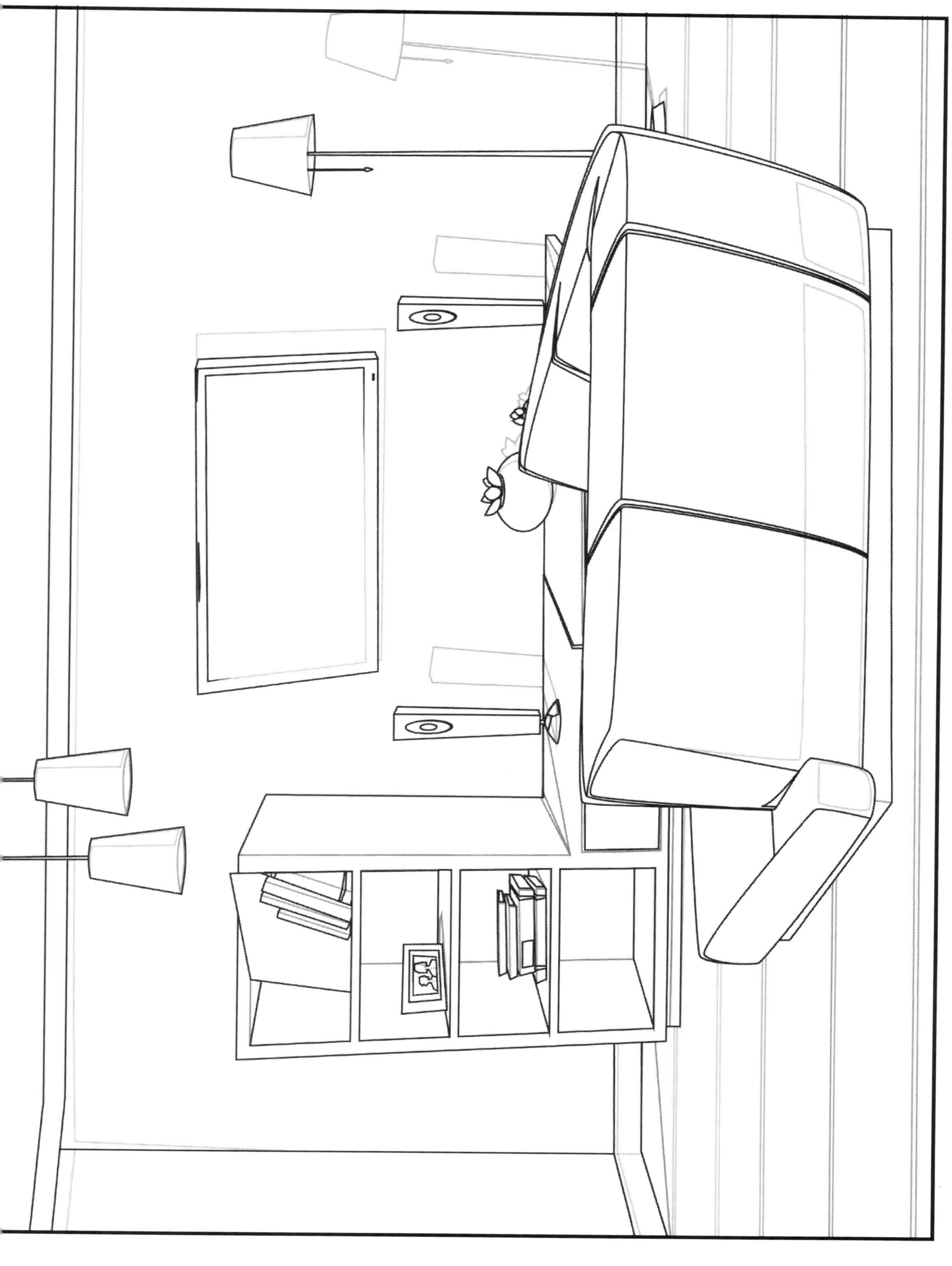

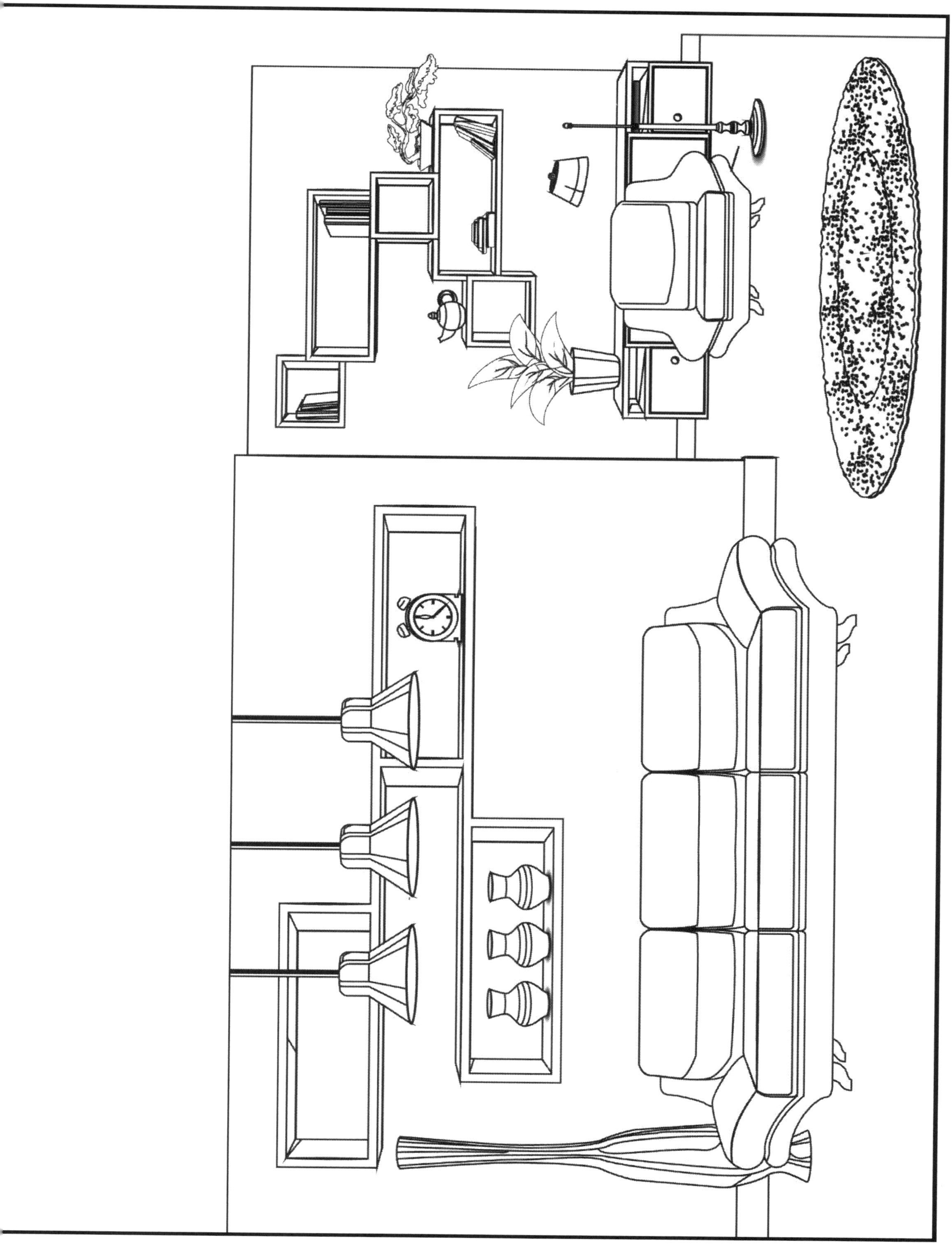

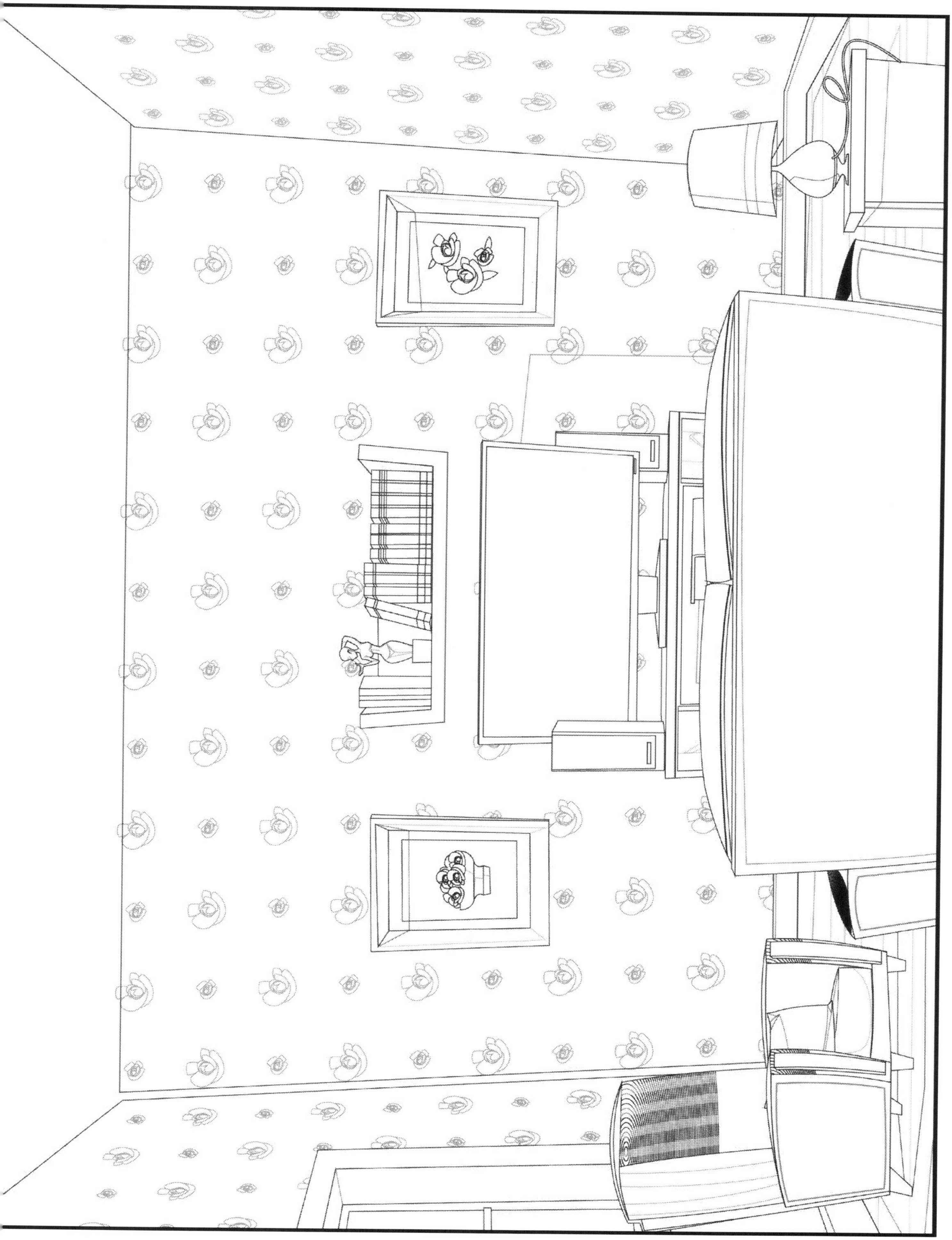

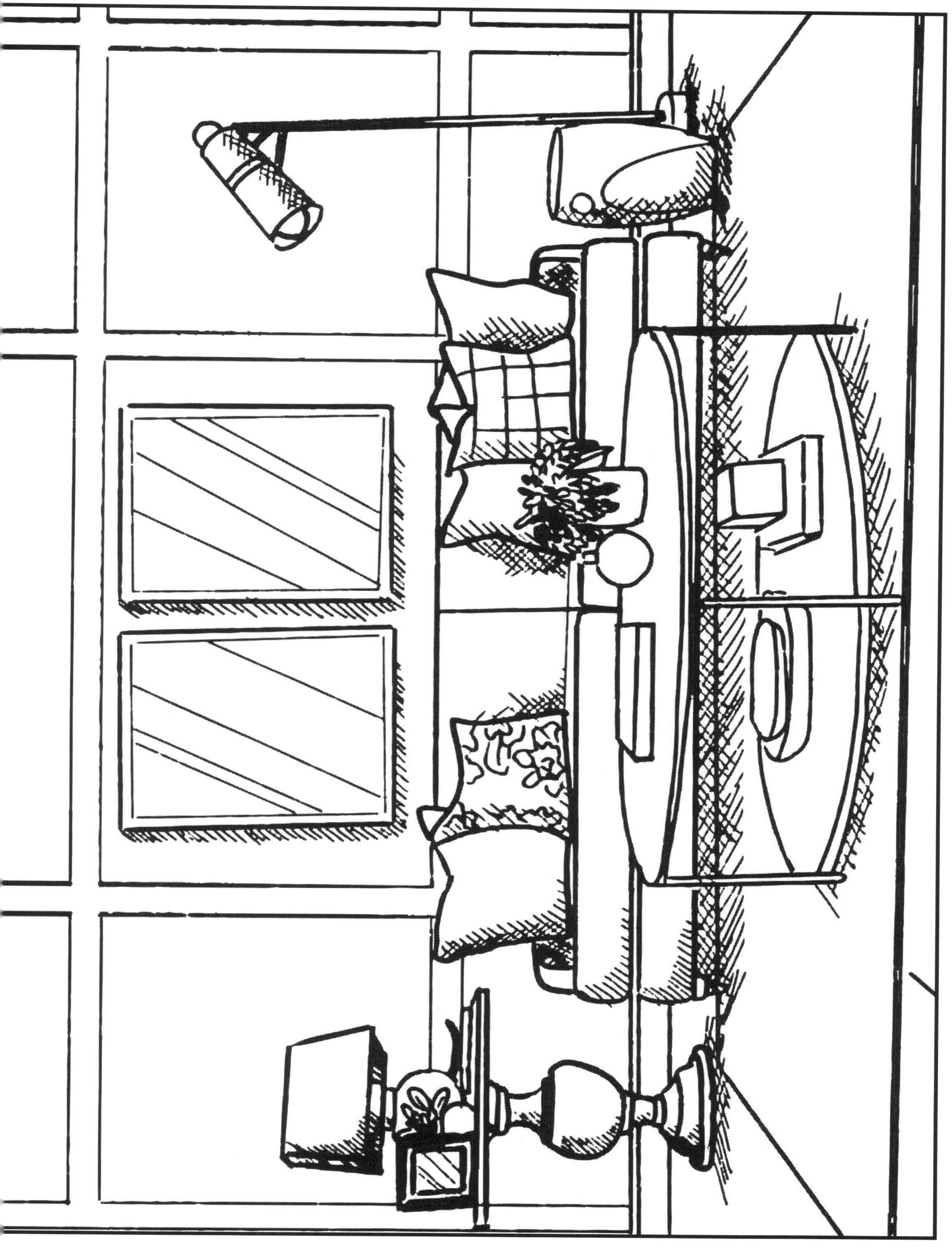

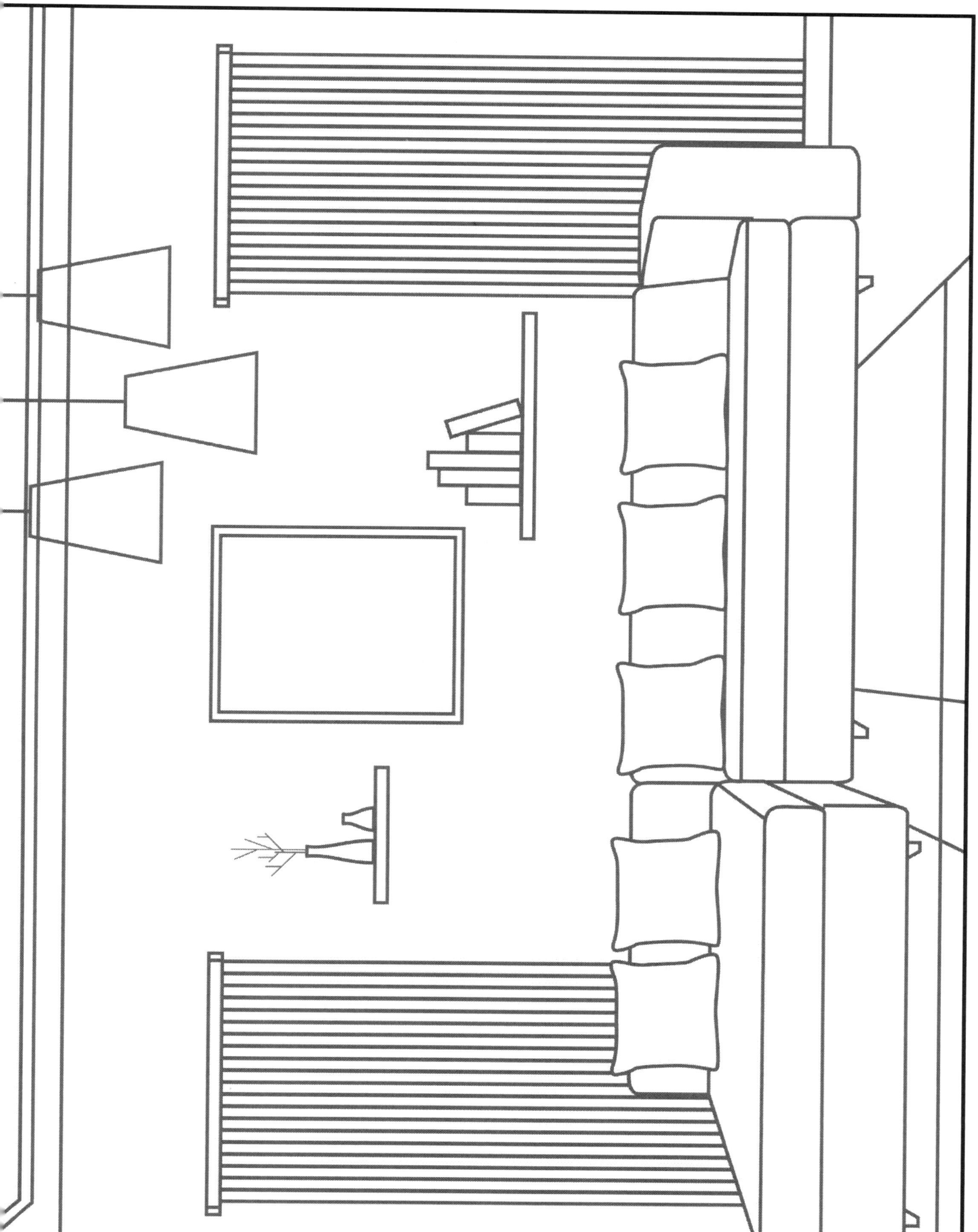

living
room

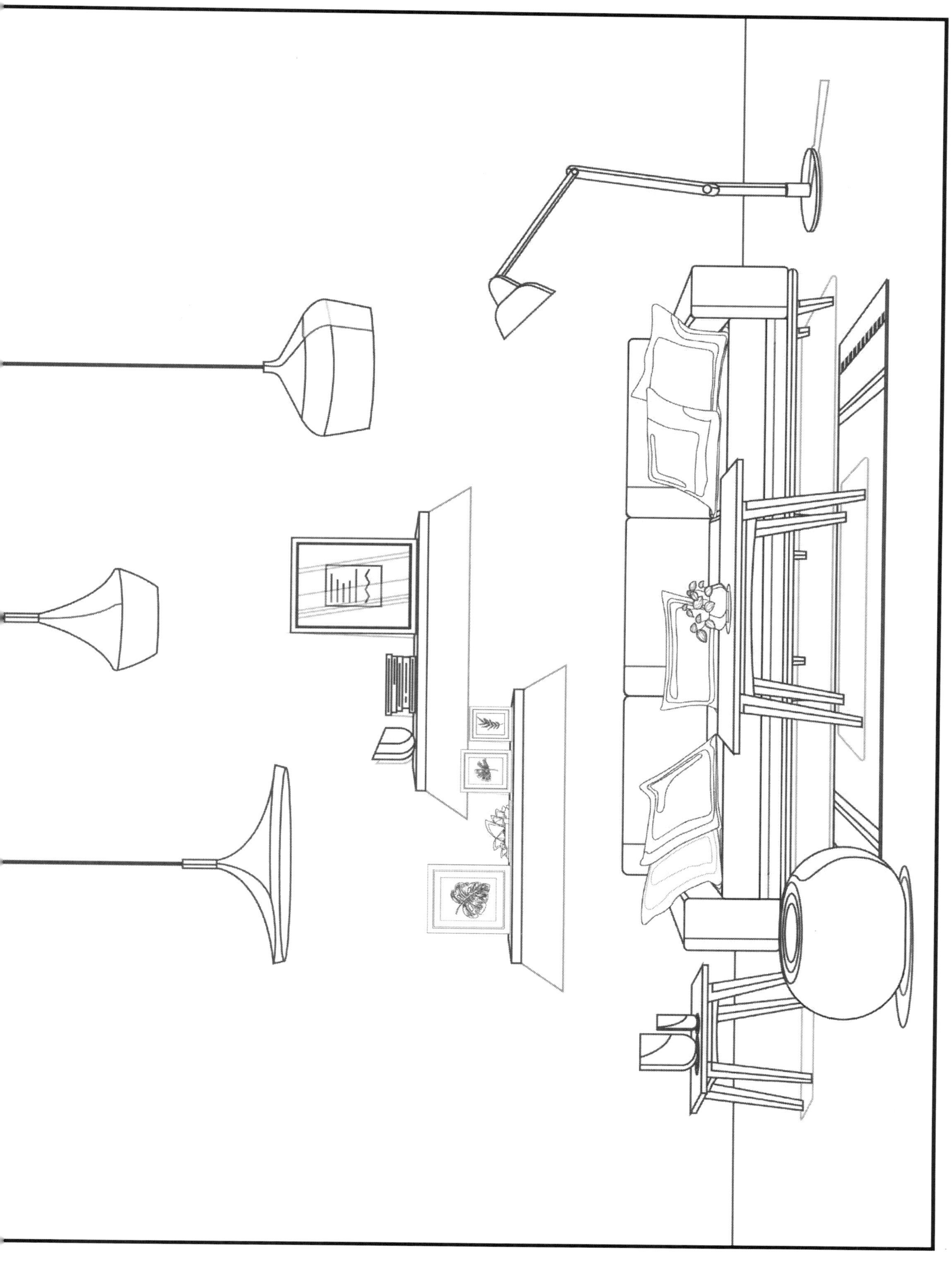

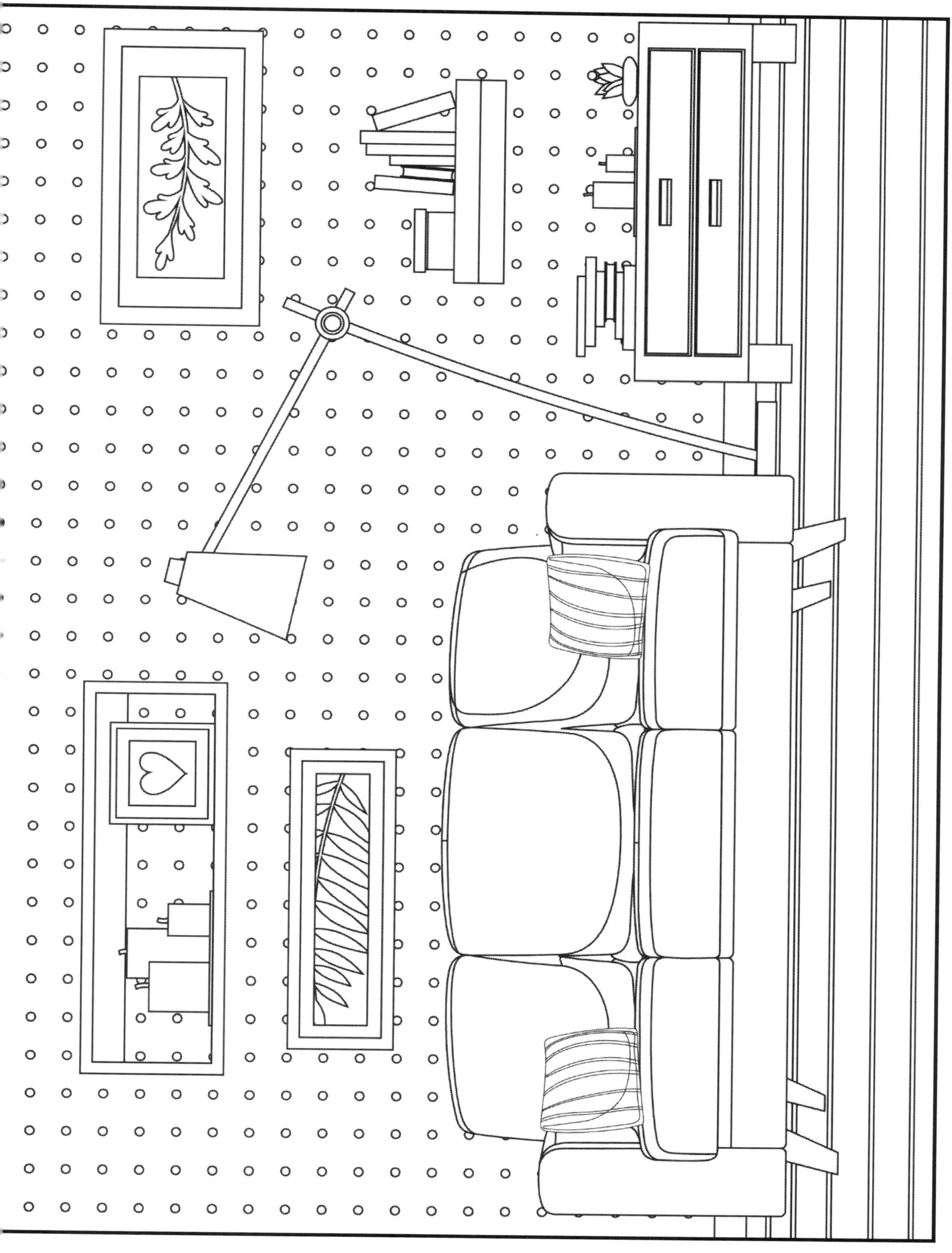

Lorem ipsum
book
BOOK

Printed in Great Britain
by Amazon

49245122R00032